This all-encompassing guide is designed to help you truly understand and appreciate the joy and significance of Easter, a cherished holiday celebrated worldwide. Whether you're a seasoned host, a first-time celebrant, or simply curious about the many facets of this special occasion, this book will serve as an invaluable resource.

Throughout the pages of "Mastering Easter," you will discover the rich history of this beloved holiday, its symbols and their meanings, as well as the fascinating traditions from around the world. We will provide you with a treasure trove of Easter wishes and toasts, accompanied by delightful classic and contemporary recipes to enjoy during your celebrations.

With "Mastering Easter" as your guide, you'll be well-equipped to plan and enjoy a memorable and meaningful holiday. From the historical roots of Easter to the practical aspects of hosting a gathering, this book will provide you with the knowledge, inspiration, and tools to fully embrace and celebrate this significant occasion.

So, dive into the pages of this ultimate Easter guide and prepare to be inspired as you embark on a journey of discovery, creativity, and celebration. Wishing you a joyous and unforgettable Easter experience!

The Story of Easter in America: A Journey Through Time

Introduction

Easter, a cherished Christian holiday, celebrates the resurrection of Jesus Christ from the dead. While its roots lie in early Christianity, the way Easter is observed has evolved over time, influenced by various cultural practices and traditions.

In this chapter, we will explore the fascinating history of Easter in the United States, taking you on a journey through time as we uncover the origins, customs, and celebrations that have shaped the holiday we know today.

Early Beginnings

Easter has its origins in the Christian tradition, which holds that Jesus Christ was crucified, buried, and resurrected around 30 A.D. The holiday's name comes from the Old English word "ēastre," which was derived from the name of an Anglo-Saxon goddess, Eostre, who represented spring and fertility.

As Christianity spread throughout Europe, early Christian leaders adopted elements from pagan spring festivals to attract more converts. These early Easter celebrations often included symbols such as eggs, which represented new life and rebirth, and rabbits, known for their fertility and rapid reproduction.

European Influences

As European settlers arrived in the New World, they brought their Easter traditions with them. In the 18th century, the Pennsylvania Dutch, who were of German descent, introduced the legend of the Easter Bunny, or "Osterhase," to America. According to this folklore, a rabbit would lay colored eggs for well-behaved children to find.

Egg decorating, a European custom that dates back to the 13th century, also became popular in America. Eastern European immigrants introduced the practice of creating intricate designs on eggs, known as pysanky, using a wax-resist technique.

The Rise of American Easter Traditions

Over time, American Easter celebrations began to develop their unique customs. In 1878, President Rutherford B. Hayes hosted the first official White House Easter Egg Roll, a tradition that continues to this day. Children gather on the White House lawn to roll eggs with a spoon, symbolizing the rolling away of the stone from Jesus' tomb.

Another beloved American Easter tradition is the Easter parade. This festive event originated in the late 19th century when affluent New Yorkers would dress in their finest clothing and stroll down Fifth Avenue after attending church services. The annual New York City Easter Parade continues to attract thousands of participants and spectators.

The Commercialization of Easter

As with many holidays, the commercialization of Easter in America began in the 19th century. Candy makers seized the opportunity to create festive treats such as chocolate bunnies, marshmallow chicks (Peeps), and colorful jelly beans. Meanwhile, greeting card companies capitalized on the holiday by producing Easter-themed cards.

The introduction of pre-packaged Easter baskets filled with toys and sweets further fueled the consumer-driven side of the holiday. Today, Easter is the second-largest candy-consuming holiday in the United States, following Halloween.

Modern American Easter Celebrations

Today, Easter in the United States is a vibrant mix of religious observance, family gatherings, and festive activities. While many Americans attend church services to commemorate the resurrection of Jesus, others enjoy secular traditions like Easter egg hunts, decorating eggs, and indulging in sweet treats.

Easter also marks the beginning of the spring season in America, with its themes of renewal, rebirth, and new life. As families gather to celebrate, they often partake in festive meals, featuring dishes such as glazed ham, deviled eggs, and hot cross buns.

Conclusion

The history of Easter in the United States is a captivating tale of tradition, cultural exchange, and the blending of ancient and modern customs. As we celebrate this beloved holiday, let us appreciate the rich tapestry of influences and practices that have shaped it over time.

From the early Christian origins to the vibrant and diverse celebrations we see today, Easter remains a cherished time for Americans to come together with family and friends, to embrace the hope and renewal of spring, and to honor the enduring spirit of this timeless holiday.

Easter Symbols in the USA: Their Stories and Significance

Easter Eggs

Easter eggs have been a significant part of Easter celebrations for centuries, symbolizing new life and rebirth. The tradition of decorating eggs dates back to the 13th century and was brought to the United States by European immigrants.

Today, Americans enjoy dyeing and decorating eggs in a variety of colors and designs. Easter egg hunts, where children search for hidden eggs, have also become a popular tradition, adding an element of fun and excitement to the holiday.

Easter Bunny

The Easter Bunny, or "Osterhase," was introduced to America by German immigrants in the 18th century. This lovable character is said to lay colored eggs for well-behaved children to find.

Over time, the Easter Bunny has evolved into a symbol of fertility and new life, as well as a popular figure in American popular culture. Today, the Easter Bunny is often depicted in movies, books, and marketing materials, and children eagerly await their visit from this beloved character each year.

Easter Baskets

Easter baskets have their roots in European harvest festivals, where farmers would bring baskets of their first crops to the church to be blessed. In America, the tradition has evolved into a more playful and commercial practice.

Parents often fill baskets with colorful eggs, sweets, toys, and other small gifts for their children to enjoy on Easter morning. This custom not only adds to the excitement of the holiday but also serves as a symbol of abundance and the blessings of spring.

Easter Lilies

The Easter Lily is a beautiful white flower that blooms in the springtime, symbolizing purity, hope, and new life. In Christian tradition, the lily is associated with the Virgin Mary and the resurrection of Jesus Christ.

Today, many Americans decorate their homes and churches with these elegant flowers during the Easter season, as a reminder of the promise of rebirth and renewal.

Hot Cross Buns

Hot cross buns are sweet, spiced bread rolls marked with a cross on top, traditionally eaten on Good Friday. The cross represents the crucifixion of Jesus, while the spices used in the recipe are said to symbolize the spices used to anoint his body after the crucifixion.

In the United States, hot cross buns have become a popular treat during the Easter season, enjoyed by many as a delicious reminder of the holiday's religious significance.

Easter Traditions Around the World: A Global Celebration

Introduction

Easter, a beloved Christian holiday, is celebrated in various ways across the globe. From unique customs and rituals to festive foods and events, each country adds its own flavor to the Easter experience.

In this chapter, we will explore some of the most fascinating and diverse Easter traditions from around the world, revealing the rich tapestry of cultures that contribute to this remarkable holiday.

Greece

In Greece, Easter is one of the most significant religious celebrations, with many unique customs. One of the most iconic is the tradition of "tsougrisma," where friends and family members tap their red-dyed eggs against each other, attempting to crack their opponent's egg without breaking their own.

The person with the last unbroken egg is considered the winner and is believed to have good luck for the year.

Italy

Easter in Italy is marked by an array of culinary delights and vibrant processions. One of the most famous events is the "Scoppio del Carro" or "Explosion of the Cart" in Florence.

A beautifully decorated cart filled with fireworks is ignited, resulting in a spectacular display. This tradition dates back over 350 years and is believed to bring a good harvest and fortune to the city.

Australia

While Australians share many common Easter traditions with other countries, they have also introduced a unique twist: the Easter Bilby. The bilby, a small marsupial native to Australia, serves as an alternative to the Easter Bunny.

This change not only raises awareness about this endangered species but also highlights the importance of conservation efforts.

Sweden and Finland

In Sweden and Finland, children often dress up as witches and go door-to-door, collecting treats in exchange for decorated willow branches or hand-drawn cards.

This tradition, known as "påskkärringar" in Sweden and "virpominen" in Finland, has its roots in the belief that witches would fly to a mountain called Blåkulla on Maundy Thursday.

Spain

Spain is well-known for its impressive Holy Week processions, particularly in the cities of Seville and Malaga. Participants, dressed in traditional hooded robes, carry ornate floats depicting scenes from the Passion of Christ.

The solemn and dramatic atmosphere of these processions draws thousands of spectators each year.

The Philippines

In the Philippines, a unique and intense Easter tradition called "Senákulo" is observed. Devout Catholics reenact the Passion of Christ, often including self-flagellation and even real-life crucifixions.

While not for the faint-hearted, these acts of penance are a powerful expression of faith for many Filipinos.

Poland

In Poland, "Śmigus-Dyngus," also known as "Wet Monday," is a lighthearted Easter tradition. On Easter Monday, people playfully splash each other with water as a symbol of cleansing and renewal.

It is also believed that girls who get soaked will marry within the year.

Conclusion

Easter traditions from around the world showcase the incredible diversity and creativity of human culture. Each country's unique customs, celebrations, and rituals offer a glimpse into the rich history and heritage that shape their communities.

By exploring these global Easter traditions, we can better appreciate the unifying power of this beloved holiday and the many ways in which people come together to celebrate the themes of hope, renewal, and new life.

The Easter Bunny: Hopping Through History

Introduction

The Easter Bunny, a beloved character in Easter celebrations, has become synonymous with the holiday in many cultures. As a symbol of new life and fertility, this endearing figure has captured the hearts of generations.

In this chapter, we will delve into the origins and evolution of the Easter Bunny, tracing its journey from ancient folklore to the cherished icon we know today.

Ancient Roots

The idea of a rabbit as a symbol of fertility dates back to antiquity. Ancient Egyptians, Greeks, and Romans revered rabbits for their rapid reproduction, which made them a natural symbol for spring, representing new life and rebirth.

The association between rabbits and springtime was further solidified by the pagan festival of Eostre, which celebrated the goddess of fertility, Eostre, for whom the hare was a sacred animal.

The Osterhase: The German Connection

The Easter Bunny as we know it today has its roots in Germanic folklore. The character, known as the "Osterhase" or "Easter Hare," was believed to lay colorful eggs for well-behaved children to find.

This tradition, which dates back to the 17th century, was brought to America by German immigrants in the 18th century, particularly those who settled in Pennsylvania, known as the Pennsylvania Dutch.

As the story goes, children would prepare nests for the Osterhase to lay its eggs in, eagerly awaiting the arrival of their colorful treasures. Over time, the Easter Bunny began to bring other treats, such as chocolates and small toys, along with the eggs.

From Folklore to Pop Culture

The Easter Bunny's popularity in America grew rapidly, fueled in part by the commercialization of the holiday in the 19th century. Confectioners seized the opportunity to create festive sweets, such as chocolate bunnies, which quickly became a staple of Easter celebrations.

The 20th century saw the Easter Bunny cement its place in American popular culture, appearing in movies, television shows, and books. By the mid-20th century, the character had evolved into a universally recognized symbol of Easter, even featuring in annual White House Easter Egg Roll celebrations.

The Modern Easter Bunny

Today, the Easter Bunny is a cherished figure in Easter celebrations across the world. The character has diversified, with various adaptations to suit different cultures and contexts. Some countries have introduced alternative characters, such as the Easter Bilby in Australia, to promote conservation efforts and raise awareness of native species.

The Easter Bunny's enduring popularity can be attributed to its universal appeal and the themes it represents, such as new life, hope, and joy. As families gather to celebrate Easter, the magical character continues to bring smiles to the faces of children and adults alike, as they partake in fun-filled activities like Easter egg hunts, bunny-shaped treats, and colorful decorations.

Conclusion

The history of the Easter Bunny is a fascinating tale of cultural evolution, blending ancient symbolism with modern customs and folklore. From its humble beginnings as a symbol of fertility and new life to the cherished character we know and love today, the Easter Bunny has captured the hearts of generations.

As we celebrate Easter each year, the enchanting figure serves as a powerful reminder of the joy, hope, and renewal that the holiday represents.

Easter Fashion and Attire: Dressing Up for the Holiday

Introduction

Easter is not only a time for religious observance and festive celebrations; it's also an occasion to dress up in our finest attire. From traditional outfits to contemporary styles, Easter fashion has always played a significant role in the holiday experience.

In this chapter, we will showcase some of the most popular Easter outfits, hats, and accessories for adults and children, highlighting the vibrant and diverse world of Easter fashion.

Traditional Easter Outfits

- **Women** have traditionally donned their best dresses for Easter celebrations. These garments often feature bright colors, floral patterns, and lightweight fabrics, reflecting the joy and renewal of the spring season. Classic accessories such as pearl necklaces, gloves, and lace-trimmed hats complete the elegant look.

- **Men** Attire often consists of a suit or a dress shirt with a tie, paired with dress pants. Lighter colors such as pastels or neutrals are popular choices for the spring season. Accessories like fedoras, dress shoes, and pocket squares add a touch of sophistication to the ensemble.

- **Children**: Little girls typically wear frilly dresses adorned with bows, lace, and floral prints, while boys dress in suits or dress shirts with ties, mimicking their adult counterparts. Children's Easter outfits often include playful elements like bunny ears, egg-shaped accessories, or pastel-colored socks and tights.

The Easter Bonnet

The Easter bonnet, a charming and timeless accessory, has been a staple of Easter fashion for centuries. Women and children alike don elaborate hats adorned with ribbons, flowers, and other embellishments to celebrate the holiday.

The tradition of the Easter bonnet can be traced back to the 19th-century Easter parades, where affluent Americans would dress in their finest clothing and stroll down Fifth Avenue in New York City after attending church services.

Contemporary Easter Fashion

Modern Easter fashion has evolved to embrace a diverse range of styles and trends. While many still opt for traditional attire, others choose more casual and contemporary outfits. Popular trends for women include flowy maxi dresses, pastel jumpsuits, or tailored blazers with floral prints.

Men might opt for pastel-colored polo shirts, linen pants, or stylish loafers. For children, rompers, graphic tees with Easter themes, and tutu skirts are trendy and fun choices.

Accessories and Finishing Touches

Accessories play a crucial role in completing an Easter outfit. Some popular options include:

- Statement jewelry: Long necklaces, bold earrings, or oversized rings can elevate an outfit and add a touch of glamour.

- Scarves and shawls: Lightweight scarves and shawls can provide both style and warmth during the cooler spring days.

- Shoes: From classic pumps and dress shoes to comfortable sandals and flats, footwear plays a vital role in completing an Easter ensemble.

- Handbags: Clutches, crossbody bags, or colorful totes can serve as both practical and stylish additions to an Easter outfit.

Conclusion

Easter fashion and attire offer a vibrant and diverse landscape of styles, ranging from traditional outfits to contemporary trends. As families gather to celebrate the holiday, dressing up in our finest clothing serves as a visual expression of the joy and renewal that the season brings.

Whether donning an elegant dress or a playful pair of bunny ears, the spirit of Easter fashion lies in embracing the holiday's themes of hope, renewal, and new life.

Eco-Friendly Easter: Celebrating the Holiday with a Green Twist

Introduction

Easter is a time of joy, renewal, and celebration. However, the holiday can also generate a significant amount of waste, from plastic eggs and decorations to excessive packaging on store-bought treats.

In this chapter, we will explore ways to celebrate Easter in a more environmentally friendly manner, focusing on sustainable practices such as using natural dyes for egg decorating and opting for eco-conscious decorations.

Natural Egg Dyes

Commercial egg dyes often contain artificial colors and chemicals that can be harmful to the environment. Instead, consider using natural dyes made from fruits, vegetables, and spices. Some examples include:

- Red/pink: Beets, raspberries, or red onion skins
- Yellow: Turmeric, saffron, or lemon peels
- Blue: Red cabbage, blueberries, or black beans
- Green: Spinach, parsley, or green tea
- Brown: Coffee, tea, or walnut shells

To prepare the natural dye, simply boil your chosen ingredient in water with a tablespoon of white vinegar for 15-30 minutes, then strain the liquid and let it cool. Soak the eggs in the dye until the desired color is achieved.

Sustainable Decorations

Instead of purchasing plastic decorations that may end up in landfills, opt for eco-friendly alternatives made from natural or recyclable materials. Some ideas include:

- DIY paper garlands: Create festive garlands from recycled paper, old magazines, or newspapers. Cut out shapes such as eggs, bunnies, or flowers and string them together.
- Reusable fabric bunting: Sew or purchase fabric bunting made from sustainable materials like organic cotton or linen. These can be used year after year, reducing waste.
- Natural centerpieces: Use fresh flowers, potted plants, or edible herbs to create beautiful, eco-friendly centerpieces for your Easter table.
- Upcycled egg cartons: Transform empty egg cartons into creative decorations or functional items, such as painted egg holders or seed starters for your spring garden.

Green Easter Baskets

Instead of buying plastic Easter baskets, consider using reusable alternatives like:

- Woven baskets: Choose baskets made from natural materials like wicker, seagrass, or bamboo.

- Cloth bags: Opt for reusable cloth bags made from organic cotton or other sustainable fabrics.

- Upcycled containers: Repurpose old containers, such as wooden boxes or metal tins, to create unique and eco-friendly Easter baskets.

Fill the baskets with sustainable gifts and treats, such as:

- Homemade sweets: Make your own chocolate eggs or cookies using organic, fair-trade ingredients.

- Wooden or fabric toys: Choose toys made from sustainable materials that can be passed down through generations.

- Seeds or seedlings: Encourage gardening by including seeds, seedlings, or small potted plants in your Easter basket.

- Recycled or eco-friendly craft supplies: Include items like recycled paper, beeswax crayons, or non-toxic playdough.

Mindful Celebrations

Finally, consider adopting eco-friendly practices in other aspects of your Easter celebrations:

- Use reusable tableware: Avoid disposable plates, cups, and utensils. Instead, use regular dinnerware, cloth napkins, and eco-friendly tablecloths.

- Plan a vegetarian or vegan menu: Incorporate more plant-based dishes into your Easter meal to reduce your environmental impact.

- Support local farmers: Purchase your Easter ingredients from local farmers or farmers' markets to minimize your carbon footprint and support your community.

- Encourage eco-friendly activities: Plan activities like planting a tree, participating in a community clean-up, or organizing a nature walk to teach children the importance of caring for the environment.

Conclusion

By embracing eco-friendly practices in our Easter celebrations, we can not only enjoy a festive holiday but also make a positive impact on the environment. From using natural dyes for egg decorating to opting for sustainable decorations, there are countless ways to reduce waste and promote a greener lifestyle.

By incorporating these ideas into our traditions, we can create a more mindful and environmentally conscious Easter experience for ourselves and future generations.

Spiritual Reflection and Meditation: Nurturing the Soul during Easter

Introduction

Easter is a time of renewal, both in nature and in spirit. While the holiday is often filled with festive celebrations, it is also an opportunity for spiritual reflection and meditation. Taking time to nurture our inner selves can deepen our understanding of the Easter message and help us cultivate a sense of gratitude, compassion, and inner peace.

In this chapter, we will explore different ways to incorporate spiritual reflection and meditation into our Easter observance, fostering a more meaningful and fulfilling holiday experience.

Prayer and Meditation

Prayer and meditation are powerful tools for connecting with our spiritual selves and cultivating a sense of inner peace. During Easter, set aside time each day to engage in quiet contemplation, either through traditional prayer or mindfulness meditation.

Consider focusing on themes such as forgiveness, renewal, hope, and gratitude. As you pray or meditate, allow yourself to be fully present in the moment, letting go of any distractions or concerns.

Reading Sacred Texts

Immersing yourself in sacred texts can provide valuable insights and inspiration during the Easter season. Whether you choose to read the Bible, the Quran, the Bhagavad Gita, or other spiritual writings, these texts can offer guidance and wisdom as you reflect on the deeper meaning of the holiday.

As you read, consider journaling your thoughts and observations, exploring how the teachings relate to your own life and spiritual journey.

Attending Spiritual Services

Many religious communities hold special services during the Easter season, offering opportunities for communal worship and reflection. Attending these gatherings can provide a sense of connection and support, fostering a deeper understanding of the holiday's spiritual significance.

Whether you are attending a traditional church service, a meditation group, or a spiritual retreat, these communal experiences can enrich your Easter observance and help you grow in your faith or spiritual practice.

Practicing Gratitude

Cultivating a grateful heart is an essential component of spiritual growth. During Easter, take time each day to acknowledge the blessings in your life, whether large or small.

You might consider keeping a gratitude journal, writing down three things you are grateful for each day, or sharing your appreciation with loved ones. By focusing on gratitude, you can foster a greater sense of contentment, joy, and connection to the divine.

Engaging in Acts of Kindness and Service

One of the most powerful ways to nurture our spiritual selves is by engaging in acts of kindness and service. During Easter, seek out opportunities to help others, whether through volunteering at a local charity, offering assistance to a neighbor in need, or simply performing small acts of kindness for those around you.

By practicing compassion and selflessness, you can cultivate a deeper sense of empathy and spiritual connection, embodying the Easter message of love and renewal.

Conclusion

Incorporating spiritual reflection and meditation into our Easter celebrations allows us to connect with the deeper meaning of the holiday and nourish our inner selves. By engaging in practices such as prayer, reading sacred texts, attending spiritual services, practicing gratitude, and serving others, we can foster a sense of spiritual growth and renewal during this transformative season.

As we nurture our souls and deepen our spiritual connections, we can experience a more profound and fulfilling Easter celebration, one that resonates with our hearts and enriches our lives.

Easter Volunteering and Charitable Giving: Sharing the Spirit of the Holiday

Introduction

Easter is a time of renewal, hope, and compassion, making it an ideal season to engage in volunteering and charitable giving. By dedicating our time, resources, and talents to helping others, we not only make a positive impact on our communities but also embody the spirit of love and generosity that lies at the heart of the Easter message.

In this chapter, we will explore various ways to participate in Easter volunteering and charitable giving, demonstrating how these acts of kindness can enrich our own lives and the lives of those around us.

Local Food Banks and Soup Kitchens

Hunger is a persistent issue in many communities, and food banks and soup kitchens rely on the support of volunteers to serve those in need. During the Easter season, consider donating non-perishable food items or volunteering your time to help prepare and serve meals.

Many organizations also host special Easter events, such as community dinners or food drives, offering additional opportunities to get involved.

Clothing Drives and Donations

As the weather warms and we transition to spring, Easter is an excellent time to clean out our closets and donate gently used clothing to those in need. Many organizations, such as homeless shelters, women's shelters, and thrift stores, accept clothing donations that directly benefit people in your community.

You can also participate in or organize a clothing drive to collect donations from friends, family, or neighbors.

Visiting Nursing Homes or Hospitals

Easter can be a lonely time for those who are confined to nursing homes or hospitals. Brighten someone's day by volunteering your time to visit with residents or patients, offering conversation, companionship, or a listening ear.

You might also consider sharing your talents, such as playing music, reading aloud, or crafting, to provide entertainment and engagement.

Supporting Children and Youth

Easter is a holiday that often focuses on children, making it a fitting time to support organizations dedicated to their well-being. Consider volunteering at a local after-school program, tutoring center, or children's hospital.

You can also donate toys, books, or art supplies to children in need or contribute to organizations that provide essential services, such as education, healthcare, and shelter.

Animal Welfare Organizations

For animal lovers, Easter is an excellent opportunity to support local animal shelters or rescue organizations. Volunteer your time to walk dogs, socialize cats, or assist with administrative tasks.

Alternatively, you can donate pet food, toys, or other supplies to support the organization's efforts to care for animals in need.

Charitable Giving

In addition to volunteering, consider making a financial donation to a charity or non-profit organization during the Easter season. Many organizations rely on the generosity of donors to fund their programs and services, making your contributions vital to their ongoing success.

You can also set up recurring donations to provide ongoing support throughout the year.

Conclusion

Participating in Easter volunteering and charitable giving not only strengthens our communities and supports those in need, but also aligns with the core values of the holiday. By giving our time, resources, and talents, we cultivate a spirit of compassion, generosity, and hope.

As we engage in acts of service and support, we not only enrich the lives of others but also deepen our own understanding of the Easter message, creating a more meaningful and fulfilling holiday experience for all.

Easter Photography Tips: Capturing Beautiful and Memorable Moments

Introduction

Easter is a time filled with joy, celebration, and precious memories. Capturing these special moments through photography allows us to preserve the essence of the holiday and cherish these memories for years to come. In this chapter, we will offer advice on taking beautiful and memorable Easter photos, from family portraits to action shots of egg hunts, ensuring that you have a collection of images that truly reflect the spirit of the occasion.

Plan Ahead

Before you start snapping photos, take some time to plan your shots. Consider the locations, backdrops, and props you want to use, as well as the timing and lighting conditions. Make sure your camera or smartphone is fully charged, and have a backup battery or charger on hand if needed.

Also, ensure that your subjects, especially children, are well-rested and fed to avoid any meltdowns during the photo session.

Use Natural Light

Natural light is often the most flattering and visually appealing choice for photography. When possible, schedule your photo sessions during the golden hours of early morning or late afternoon when the light is soft and warm. If you're shooting indoors, choose a location with plenty of natural light, such as near a large window or a well-lit room.

Capture Candid Moments

While posed portraits have their place, candid shots can capture the genuine emotions and interactions that make Easter special.

Keep your camera ready and be prepared to capture those unexpected moments, such as a child's excitement during an egg hunt or a heartfelt hug between family members. These candid shots often become the most treasured memories of the day.

Get Creative with Angles and Perspectives

Experiment with different angles and perspectives to create more dynamic and interesting images. Try shooting from a low angle to emphasize a child's excitement during an egg hunt, or capture a bird's-eye view of a beautifully decorated Easter table.

Don't be afraid to move around and explore different vantage points to find the perfect shot.

Focus on Details

Easter is filled with charming details, from decorated eggs and festive treats to colorful outfits and decorations. Be sure to capture these elements in your photographs to tell the complete story of your Easter celebrations.

Use a macro or close-up setting on your camera to highlight the intricate patterns on an egg or the delicate petals of a spring flower.

Incorporate Props and Backdrops

Props and backdrops can add a fun and festive touch to your Easter photos. Consider using items like Easter baskets, pastel-colored balloons, or a floral wreath as props in your images.

For backdrops, think about using natural elements like a blooming garden, a rustic wooden fence, or a simple fabric background in soft, spring colors.

Take Action Shots

Easter activities like egg hunts, egg rolling, or games provide excellent opportunities for action shots. Use a fast shutter speed or sports mode on your camera to capture sharp, in-focus images of moving subjects.

Also, consider using burst mode to take multiple shots in rapid succession, increasing your chances of capturing the perfect moment.

Edit and Organize Your Photos

Once you've captured your Easter memories, spend some time editing and organizing your images. Use photo editing software or apps to enhance colors, adjust lighting, and crop your images for the best composition.

Finally, create an album or digital gallery to store and display your favorite Easter photos, making it easy to revisit and share these cherished memories.

Conclusion

Capturing beautiful and memorable Easter photos is a rewarding way to preserve the spirit and joy of the holiday. By planning ahead, using natural light, experimenting with angles, and focusing on details, you can create a collection of images that truly reflect the essence of your Easter celebrations.

With these photography tips in mind, you'll be well-equipped to capture stunning family portraits, action shots of egg hunts, and all the special moments that make Easter a time to remember. So, grab your camera or smartphone and start snapping, creating a visual record of your Easter memories that you and your loved ones can cherish for years to come.

Bonus: Easter Gift ideas

Introduction

Easter is a time of celebration, renewal, and togetherness, making it the perfect occasion to share thoughtful gifts with friends and family.

Whether you're looking for traditional Easter treats or unique and personalized presents, our selection of Easter gift ideas will help you find the perfect way to show your love and appreciation this holiday season

Personalized Easter Baskets

Create a custom Easter basket filled with a variety of goodies tailored to the recipient's interests and preferences.

This can include chocolate eggs, candy, small toys, books, art supplies, or self-care items. Personalize the basket itself with the recipient's name, initials, or a unique design.

Decorated Easter Eggs

Hand-decorated Easter eggs make beautiful and memorable gifts. Choose from traditional dyed eggs, painted wooden eggs, or even delicate blown-out eggs decorated with intricate designs. Personalize the eggs with the recipient's name or a special message for an extra special touch.

Easter-Themed Cookie Decorating Kit

An Easter-themed cookie decorating kit is a fun and interactive gift for kids and adults alike. Include pre-baked cookies shaped like Easter eggs, bunnies, or chicks, along with colorful icing, sprinkles, and other edible decorations.

Springtime Floral Arrangement

A beautiful bouquet or arrangement of spring flowers, such as tulips, daffodils, or hyacinths, makes a lovely and fragrant Easter gift. Choose a mix of pastel colors that evoke the spirit of the season, and consider adding a decorative vase or container for an extra special touch.

DIY Easter Craft Kit

Give the gift of creativity with a DIY Easter craft kit. Include all the necessary materials and instructions for the recipient to create their own Easter-themed decorations, such as felt bunnies, egg ornaments, or a festive wreath.

Personalized Jewelry

For a more lasting and personal gift, consider custom jewelry, such as a necklace or bracelet with the recipient's initials, name, or a special message. Choose a design that reflects the Easter theme, such as a cross, egg, or bunny charm.

Gourmet Easter Treats

Delight the taste buds with gourmet Easter treats, such as artisanal chocolate eggs, high-quality candy, or homemade baked goods. Present these treats in a decorative box or container to make the gift feel even more special.

Easter Storybook or Devotional

Share the story of Easter with a beautifully illustrated children's book, or provide spiritual nourishment with a daily devotional or inspirational book focused on the Easter season.

Between, This book is good option.

Plush Easter Toys

Soft and cuddly plush toys, such as bunnies, chicks, or lambs, make adorable Easter gifts for children of all ages. Choose a toy that is age-appropriate and consider adding personalization with the child's name or initials.

Experience Gifts

Create lasting memories with an experience gift, such as tickets to a local event, a family outing, or a special Easter-themed activity like an egg hunt or a visit to a petting zoo.

Conclusion

With these Easter gift ideas in mind, you can create thoughtful and festive presents that will delight and surprise your loved ones this holiday season.

From personalized Easter baskets to springtime floral arrangements, these gifts will help you share the joy and warmth of the Easter season with those who matter most to you.

Bonus: DIY receipts

DIY Easter Egg Decorating

Materials:

- Hard-boiled eggs or plastic eggs
- Food coloring or natural dyes (such as beet juice or turmeric)
- White vinegar
- Stickers, washi tape, or paint markers
- Rubber bands, string, or masking tape for creating patterns

Instructions:

Create various dye baths by mixing food coloring or natural dyes with water and a splash of white vinegar in separate bowls. Dip eggs in the dye baths to achieve the desired colors. Use stickers, tape, rubber bands, or paint markers to create patterns and designs on the eggs.

Handmade Easter Cards

Materials:

- Cardstock or pre-made blank cards
- Colored paper or construction paper
- Scissors
- Glue
- Markers, colored pencils, or crayons
- Stickers, ribbons, or other embellishments (optional)

Instructions:

Cut out various Easter-themed shapes, such as eggs, bunnies, or flowers, from colored paper. Arrange and glue the shapes onto the cardstock or blank cards. Decorate with markers, colored pencils, or crayons, and add stickers or other embellishments as desired.

Easter Bunny Garland

Materials:
- Colored paper or cardstock
- Scissors
- Hole punch
- String or ribbon
- Glue
- Cotton balls or pom-poms (optional)

Instructions:

Cut out bunny shapes from colored paper or cardstock. Punch holes in the ears of each bunny, and thread the string or ribbon through the holes to create a garland. Optionally, glue cotton balls or pom-poms to the bunnies as tails.

Paper Plate Easter Basket

Materials:
- Paper plates
- Scissors
- Stapler or glue
- Markers, crayons, or paint
- Ribbon or pipe cleaners (optional)

Instructions:

Fold a paper plate in half and cut two slits along the folded edge, leaving an inch or two uncut on each end. Open the paper plate and fold the cut sections inward to form the sides of the basket. Secure the sides with staples or glue. Decorate the basket with markers, crayons, or paint, and add a ribbon or pipe cleaner handle if desired.

Clothespin Easter Bunny

Materials:
- Wooden clothespins
- White and pink acrylic paint
- Paintbrushes
- Small googly eyes
- Pink pom-poms
- White pipe cleaners
- Glue

Instructions:
Paint the clothespins with white acrylic paint and let them dry. Paint a small pink heart shape on the top half of each clothespin to represent the bunny's nose. Glue googly eyes above the nose and a pink pom-pom below the nose for the tail. Cut white pipe cleaners into small pieces and bend them to form bunny ears. Glue the ears onto the top of the clothespin.

Bonus: Best Easter Wishes

Wishing you a joyful and egg-ceptional Easter filled with love and happiness!

May the Easter Bunny bring you and your family an abundance of joy, love, and chocolates.

Hoppy Easter! May your day be filled with laughter, love, and plenty of Easter egg hunts.

Wishing you a basket full of blessings and a springtime filled with new beginnings.

Easter is here, and so is new life and hope. Have a blessed and meaningful Easter!

May the miracle of Easter brighten your days with love, happiness, and the warmth of spring.

Celebrate this Easter with a heart filled with love and gratitude. Happy Easter!

Sending you egg-stra special Easter wishes for a day filled with love, happiness, and family.

Wishing you and your loved ones a joyful Easter, filled with hope, renewal, and new beginnings.

Hop on over for a cracking good time this Easter! Wishing you an eggs-traordinary day.

May the Easter Bunny hop into your life with a basket full of happiness and blessings.

Enjoy the beauty of springtime and the blessings of Easter with your loved ones.

Wishing you a fun-filled Easter with lots of love, chocolate bunnies, and new memories.

Here's to a hoppin' good Easter filled with family, love, and lots of chocolate eggs!

May the spirit of Easter fill your heart with joy and your home with warmth and love.

Wishing you an egg-citing Easter surrounded by the love of friends and family.

Hoping your Easter is filled with love, laughter, and a whole lot of chocolate!

May this Easter bring you endless blessings, boundless love, and countless chocolate eggs.

Sending you warm Easter wishes for a bright and beautiful spring season ahead.

Wishing you a joyful Easter filled with colorful eggs, chocolate bunnies, and the love of family.

May your Easter be filled with the sweetest moments and the happiest memories.

Celebrate this Easter with love in your heart and a spirit of gratitude.

Wishing you a blessed Easter filled with hope, joy, and the promise of new beginnings.

May your Easter basket be filled with love, joy, and all the good things in life.

Sending you warm and heartfelt Easter wishes for a joyful and blessed celebration.

Enjoy a fun and memorable Easter with your loved ones, filled with laughter and love.

Wishing you a blessed and beautiful Easter, surrounded by family, friends, and plenty of chocolate!

Hoping your Easter is as sweet as the chocolate eggs and as colorful as the painted ones.

Celebrate the miracle of Easter with a heart full of peace, joy, and love.

Wishing you a happy Easter filled with hope, renewal, and the spirit of spring.

Here's to an eggs-tra special Easter filled with love, laughter, and good times.

May the joy of Easter bloom in your heart like a beautiful springtime flower.

Wishing you a delightful Easter with family, friends, and a heart full of happiness.

Sending you the warmest Easter greetings for a day filled with love, joy, and togetherness.

May your Easter be filled with the magic of new beginnings and the promise of brighter days.

Wishing you a blessed Easter filled with love, happiness, and the renewal of spring.

Hoping your Easter is egg-stra special, just like you!

Wishing you a beautiful Easter filled with love, joy, and the gift of family.

Celebrate this Easter with hope in your heart, love in your soul, and joy in your life.

May the beauty of spring and the spirit of Easter bring you happiness and cherished moments.

Wishing you a blessed Easter filled with the warmth of family, the joy of renewal, and the hope of brighter days.

May your Easter be sprinkled with love, happiness, and the sweetest memories.

Sending you an abundance of love and blessings this Easter season.

Wishing you a joyful and memorable Easter with your loved ones, filled with love, laughter, and gratitude.

Here's to an egg-stra special Easter celebration filled with family, friends, and a heart full of warmth.

May the promise of Easter fill your life with hope, love, and new beginnings.

Wishing you an Easter filled with hope, joy, and the magic of springtime.

Enjoy a blessed and joyful Easter, surrounded by love, laughter, and the beauty of spring.

Hoping your Easter is filled with sweet surprises, love, and happiness to last the whole year through.

Bonus: Easter calendar for next 10 years

Catholic Easter Dates

2023: April 9

2024: March 31

2025: April 20

2026: April 5

2027: March 28

2028: April 16

2029: April 1

2030: April 21

2031: April 13

2032: March 28

Please note that these dates are based on the Gregorian calendar for Catholic Easter. While the dates may vary slightly depending on the region and specific church, these should provide a general idea of when Easter will be celebrated in the coming years.

Orthodox Easter Dates

2023: April 16

2024: May 5

2025: April 20

2026: April 12

2027: May 2

2028: April 16

2029: April 8

2030: April 28

2031: April 13

2032: May 2

Please note that these dates are based on the Julian calendar for Orthodox Easter. While the dates may vary slightly depending on the region and specific church, these should provide a general idea of when Easter will be celebrated in the coming years.

A Complete Easter Guide: Celebrate with Confidence

In this comprehensive guide, we've covered everything you need to know about Easter, making it the ultimate manual for anyone seeking to fully embrace and celebrate this cherished holiday. From the rich history and symbolism of Easter to a wide array of festive wishes, toasts, recipes, and crafts, this book provides all the tools and inspiration you need to make the most of your Easter celebrations.

We've explored Easter traditions from around the world, delved into the origins of the beloved Easter Bunny, and provided practical tips for capturing beautiful and memorable photographs during your festivities. Additionally, we've shared ideas for eco-friendly and charitable ways to observe the holiday, along with suggestions for fashionable and trendy attire.

With this complete Easter guide in hand, you'll be well-equipped to plan and enjoy a memorable and meaningful holiday, no matter your background or experience. Whether you're hosting a gathering with family and friends or celebrating quietly at home, this book will serve as a valuable resource to help you fully appreciate the joy and significance of the Easter season.

We hope that the information, tips, and ideas in this book enrich your Easter celebrations and bring warmth, happiness, and a sense of renewal to you and your loved ones. May your Easter be filled with love, laughter, and cherished memories that last a lifetime.

Contents